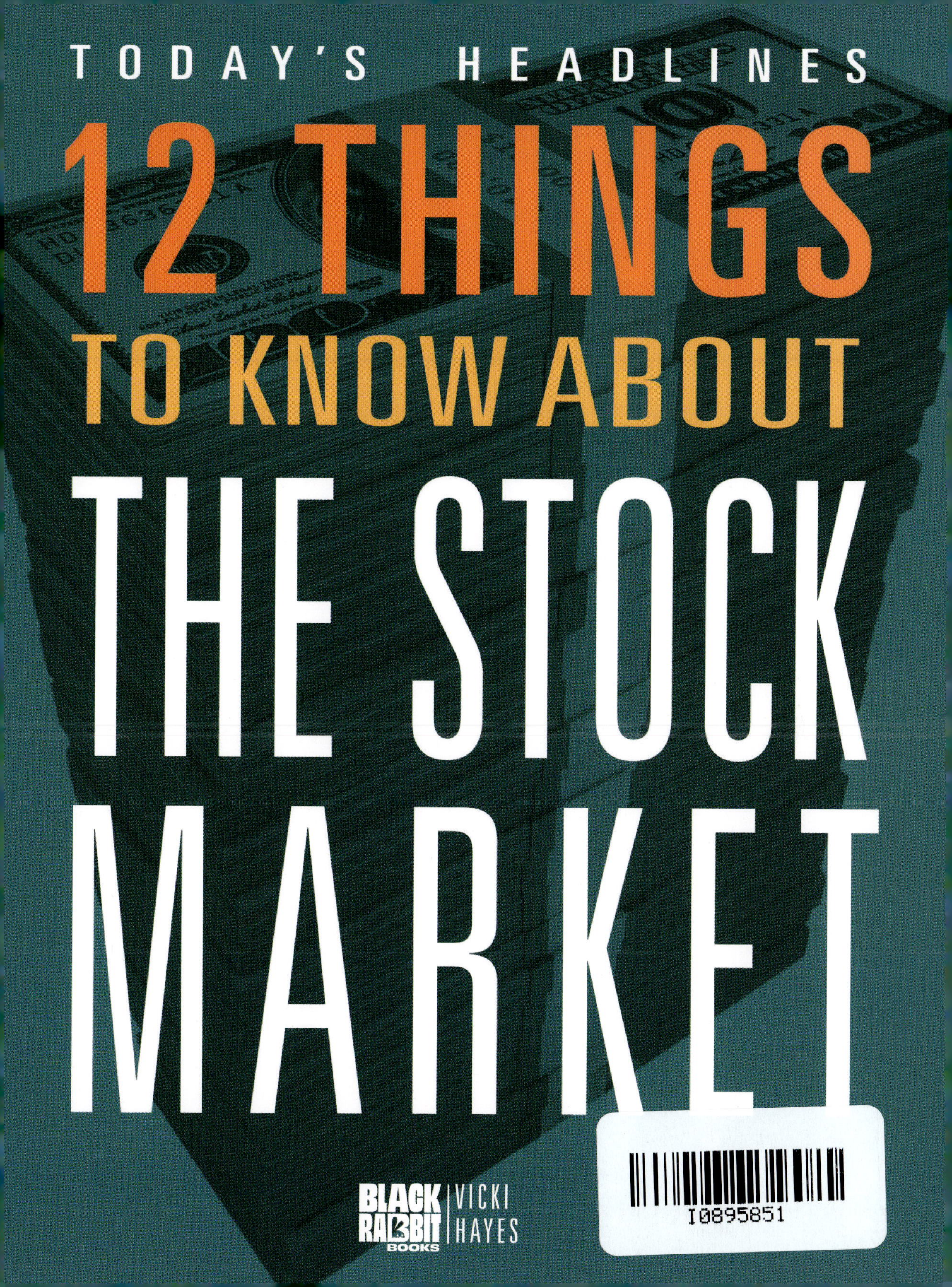

TODAY'S HEADLINES

12 THINGS TO KNOW ABOUT THE STOCK MARKET

BLACK RABBIT BOOKS

VICKI HAYES

I0895851

Table of Contents

The New York Stock Exchange (NYSE) is one of the most well known American stock exchanges.

The Stock Market Is Not a *Physical Place*

1

The stock market is where people buy and sell stocks. Stocks are also called **shares**. Owning a company's stock represents owning a part of the company. Companies sell these shares to get money for their businesses. People buy these shares to earn money. But the stock market is not an actual place. You can't visit it. It is a network or system.

A purchase of 100 or more shares is called a round lot.

Companies that want to sell stock are listed on a stock exchange. Some stock exchanges are places you can visit. The New York Stock Exchange (NYSE) is in New York City. Many exchanges are electronic. They can be used online.

People who buy stocks are called investors. Buying and selling stocks is called trading. Investors can trade anywhere. A Los Angeles investor can trade in China. A Japanese investor can trade in London.

When investors buy stock, they are buying part of a company. The company uses the money to make their business better. Investors hope this happens. Then their stocks are worth more.

Stock prices can go up and down over a course of days.

Stock market numbers can quickly change.

$18.9 billion Average daily value of stocks traded on the New York Stock Exchange.

The stock market is more than 400 years old. • The United States makes up 42 percent of the world stock market. • You must be at least 18 to invest in stocks.

There Is More Than One *Stock Exchange*

2

Countries around the world invest in the stock market. Many have one or more stock exchanges. Some are bigger than others. The NYSE is one of the biggest. It is on Wall Street in New York City. The London Stock Exchange in England is another big market. So is the Tokyo Stock Exchange in Japan. They list most of the world's companies. Trading on stock exchanges usually happens during business hours. The NYSE trades Monday through Friday from 9:30 AM to 4 PM eastern time.

Wall Street is the financial district of New York City.

The NYSE is in a building. Many of its trades happen in person. But this is becoming more unusual. A second big stock exchange in the United States is the NASDAQ. This stands for National Association of

Built in 1903, the NYSE Building has a classical look with columns and stone.

Think About It

Do you like working with computers and numbers? Would you like working at a stock exchange?

Securities Dealers Automatic Quotation System. All NASDAQ trades occur electronically.

Companies choose where to list their stock. Each exchange has different benefits. Some offer financial protections. Some require financial advisors. Also, stock exchanges can choose the companies they list. They don't want companies that might be bad **investments**.

60 Number of major global stock exchanges.

In 2020, NASDAQ said their listed companies had to have at least one woman and one minority on their boards. • Robots make 90 percent of stock trades. • The Shanghai Stock Exchange takes a 1.5-hour lunch break.

An electronic billboard in Times Square shows NASDAQ numbers.

Owning a Stock Is Owning a Piece *of a Company*

3

People save money in different ways. Some people use savings accounts. Money is safe and will earn interest in these accounts. Other people use stocks. Stocks could earn more money than a savings account. But stocks could also lose money. That makes them riskier. To make money, investors need to buy stocks at a low price. Then they sell those stocks at a higher price. But sometimes this is not possible. Then investors lose money.

Investors can look at a company's listing on a stock exchange. The listing tells them about the company's profits. It shows the losses too. The profile also includes the company's business plan to make money. This helps investors decide which stocks to buy.

But investors cannot buy stocks themselves. They have to use a broker. A broker has a special license to buy and sell stocks. Investors tell their brokers what they want to buy. The broker makes the purchase. It can be online, over the phone, or in person. Sales are made differently at each stock exchange.

Traders also buy and sell stocks. But traders usually work for large firms. Brokers work for individual investors. Investors should have a strategy when buying stock. How many shares will they buy? Will they buy them all at once? At what price will they buy them? Investors give these directions to brokers. Investors also give directions to brokers about when to sell.

Think About It Are you a risk taker? Stocks can earn you a lot of money. But you may also lose money. How would you invest your money?

300 Number of traders on the floor of the NYSE in 2023.

If an investor thinks a company is going to do well, then they should buy stock. • The price of a stock can go up and down for many reasons. • Stockbrokers say September is the worst month to trade stocks. The best month is April.

Some finance newspapers track daily stock prices in a stock table.

The First Stock Exchange *Was in Amsterdam*

4

Moneylenders have been around since the Middle Ages. Back in the 1300s, they would meet in the market square. They would loan money to people. They would invest in local businesses. Some lenders did business in other towns. Some grew their businesses into other countries.

The Amsterdam Stock Exchange is based in the Netherlands.

The Dutch East India Company was a trading company. They owned sailing ships. They shipped goods from the Far East to Europe. In 1602, the company wanted to expand. They needed money. They came up with an idea. They would sell pieces of the company to investors. This made investors part-owners of the company. If the company did well, the investors shared in the profit. If the company did poorly, the investors lost their money. At first, the Dutch East India Company sold shares in coffee houses. But they needed an organized marketplace. This became the Amsterdam Stock Exchange.

The Amsterdam Stock Exchange was successful. Many shares were bought and sold there. Many people made a lot of money. Over the next 200 years, stock exchanges were set up around the world. London, New York, Tokyo, and Shanghai each created their own exchange.

78 million Value of the East India Co. in Dutch guilders in 1637 ($7.9 trillion).

The Amsterdam Stock Exchange was created in 1611. • In 1790, the first US stock exchange started in Philadelphia. • Women first worked on the NYSE trading floor in 1943.

BUTTONWOOD TREE AGREEMENT It was the late 1700s in New York. A group of men met every day. They gathered under a buttonwood tree. They bought and sold stocks. Soon, they decided to make rules about how to trade stock. This was called the Buttonwood Tree Agreement. Eventually, this became the New York Stock Exchange. The NYSE is the largest in the world.

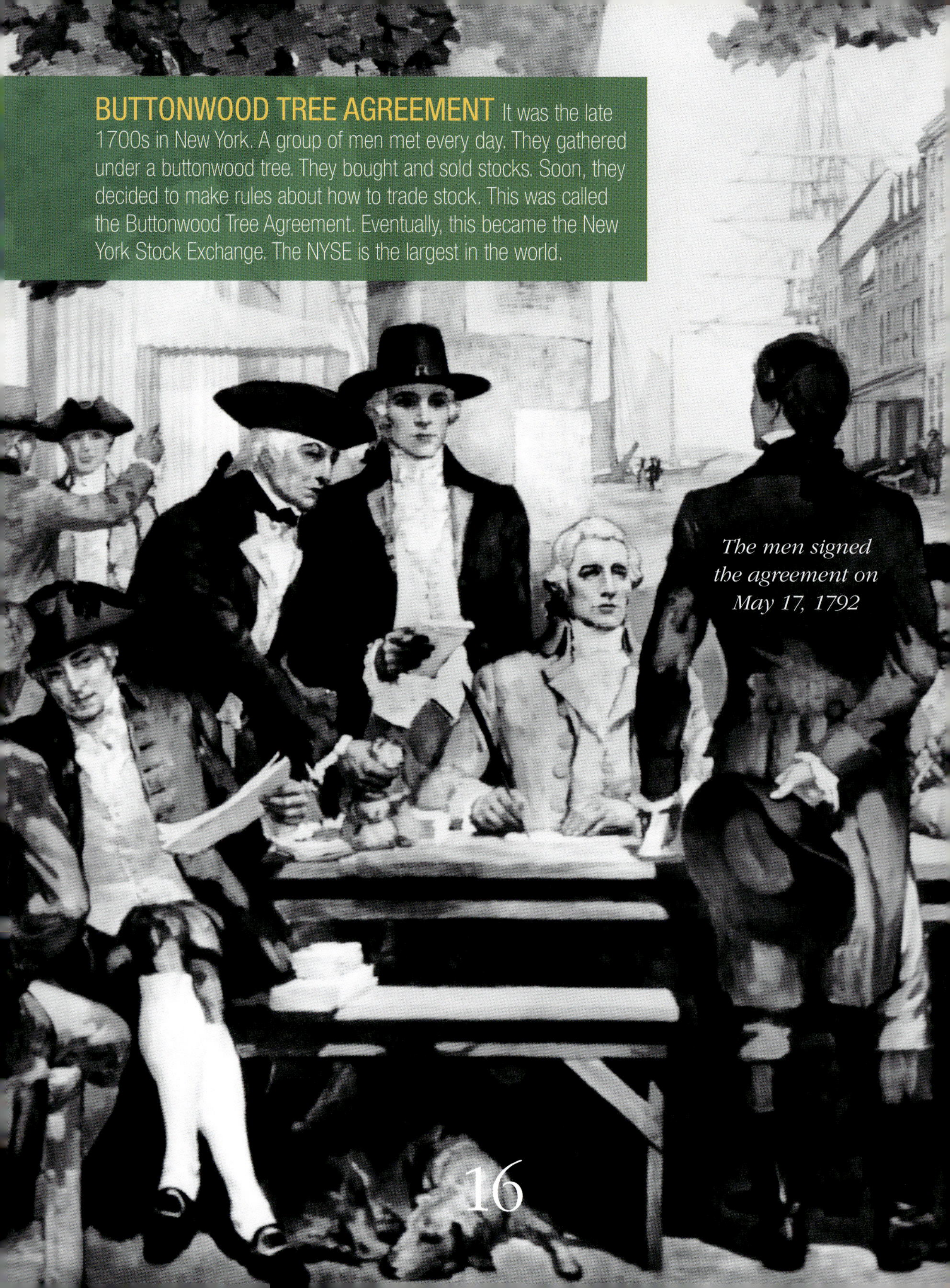

The men signed the agreement on May 17, 1792

The Stock Market's Purpose Is *to Raise Money*

5

Companies need money to do business. They need money for machines and equipment. They need to pay employees. They must buy supplies. But what if a company does not have enough money? One thing it can do is sell shares of stock.

A private company can sell shares to private investors. The investors become stockholders. Stockholders may want to sell shares to public investors. This means the company has to go public. The first time a company sells public shares, it is called an initial public offering (IPO).

An IPO is a big step for a company. It's a chance to raise a lot of money. But the company must be ready. It must be worth around $1 billion. And it must meet other requirements. The requirements are made by the SEC. The SEC is the Securities and Exchange Commission.

In an IPO, the company lists its shares on the stock exchange. The shares can be bought by the public. Stocks often have a low price during an IPO. This attracts a lot of investors. Only about 20 percent of IPOs succeed. The rest fail. A failure means the company didn't raise enough money to grow. They may have failed to produce what they said they would. Or the product wasn't as good as they promised. The company's stocks are worth less than when the investors bought them.

The SEC oversees IPOs and enforces the laws that govern the stock exchange.

154 Number of IPOs on the US stock market in 2023.

Microsoft had a successful IPO in 1986. • Microsoft's initial share price was $21. That increased to $31.50 by the end of the day. • About 2.5 million shares were sold the first day. Microsoft raised $61 million.

IPO

The stock market usually goes up over time.

Many People Work in the *Stock Market*

6

Buying and selling stocks is not the only thing that happens in the stock market. Companies are **audited**, or checked. Computers are programmed and maintained. Software is developed. Consultant teams are formed.

Stockbrokers buy and sell stock. They do this for their clients. Some brokers offer advice. They tell their clients what stocks to trade. Brokers usually have college degrees. They study business or accounting. This training helps them get clients. Brokers must also pass an exam to get a license.

Market makers also buy and sell stocks. But their work is a little different. A market maker trades stocks for financial companies or big banks. They hold shares of lots of companies. They are always ready to trade. This helps to keep the stock market working.

Analysts also have an important job. They study companies. They look at business trends. They try to figure out which stocks are good to trade. Then they give advice to brokers. There are officers who enforce the rules and laws of the market. An economist studies global issues related to the stock market. There are also lower-level jobs. These are assistants, managers, and clerks. They are support people. Or they are in training for higher level jobs.

WALL STREET

Wall Street is in New York City. It is one of the most famous streets in the world. It is the home of the New York Stock Exchange. When the NYSE started in 1792, Wall Street was just a dusty road. Today, it is the financial center of the globe.

$86,110 Average salary for a New York stockbroker in 2024.

Working in the stock market can be stressful. The job is fast-paced and has long hours. • In 2024, 14 percent of US stockbrokers were women. • To become a broker, get a college degree. Then do an internship and pass the exams.

Stock brokers bid against each other to buy stock.

There Is No Set Price *for Stocks*

7

How much do stocks cost? That depends on what a buyer is willing to pay. An investor may want to sell their stocks for $100 per share. But that does not mean they will. The highest bid for their stocks might only be $75 per share. If the seller doesn't like this, they can wait. They can wait days, weeks, or years. The price of their stocks might go up. Or it might not.

Buying and selling stocks is risky business. **Free market** forces decide how much a stock is worth. For example, you have a baseball card that no one else has. A lot of people are interested in buying it. You can charge a high price for that card. But what if you have a card no one wants? Then the price of the card goes down. This is supply and demand. Supply is how much of something there is. Demand is how many people want it.

ChatGPT is a chatbot developed by OpenAI.

There are many reasons people want to own part of a company. One reason is if they think its products are going to be successful. In 2022, a company called OpenAI released a new product. It was called ChatGPT. At that time, one share of OpenAI was selling for $63.19. Within a year, a share sold for $184.87. The product was exciting to people. They thought it would do well. People wanted to own shares of the company.

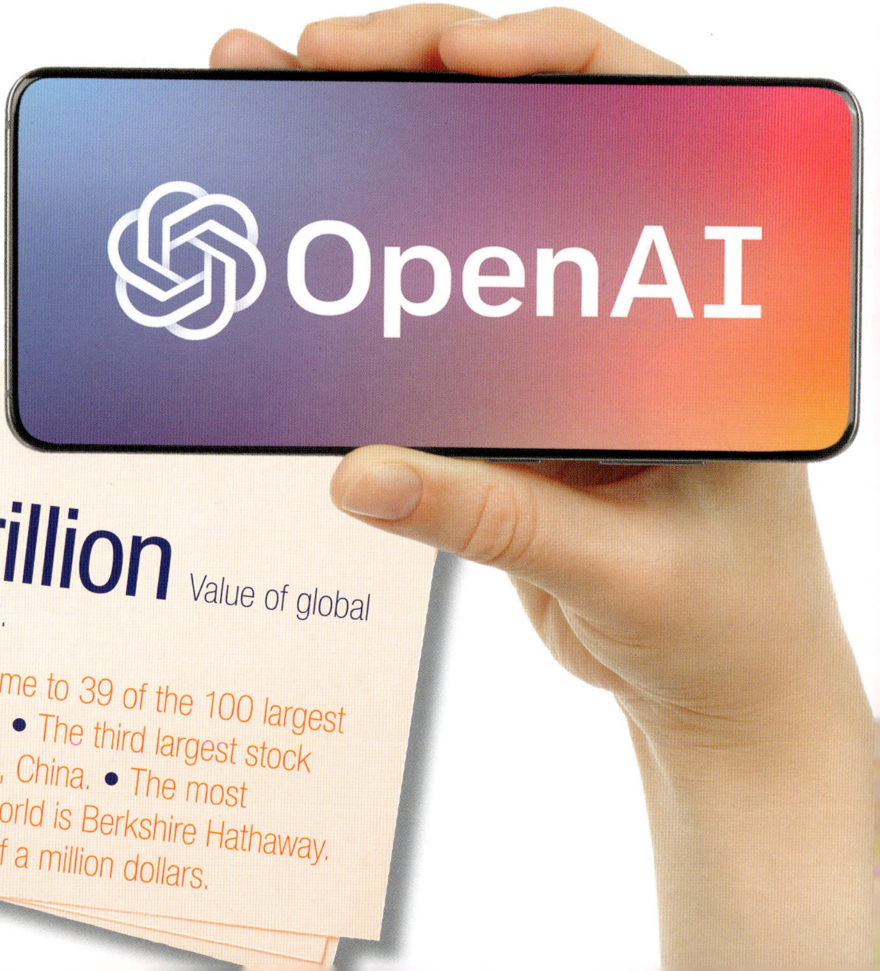

$109 trillion Value of global stock markets in 2023.

The United States is home to 39 of the 100 largest companies in the world. • The third largest stock exchange is in Shanghai, China. • The most expensive stock in the world is Berkshire Hathaway. One share costs over half a million dollars.

Stock Averages Show How Strong *the Market Is*

8

The stock market is not the only place to invest money. Investors can buy and sell **real estate**. Or they can buy and sell government **bonds**. Investors decide where to put their money. They look at how well certain investments are doing. Sometimes real estate is the best place to invest. Other times the stock market is the best place to invest.

Charles Dow wanted to help with this. He wanted to show investors how strong the stock market was. In 1896, he took 12 stocks and averaged the prices. Then he charted the averages over time. His charts showed trends in the stock prices. The charts helped investors know when to buy or sell. Dow's charts became known as the Dow Jones Industrial Average (DJIA).

Today, investors use several stock averages. One of the best-known is the DJIA. There is also the S&P 500. And there is the NASDAQ Composite Index. Over the years, stocks have changed. Companies may **split** stocks. They may switch one stock for another. All of this means stock prices are averaged often. It must be done very carefully too.

30 Number of companies whose stocks are tracked on the DJIA in 2024.

The S&P 500 averages the stock prices of 500 companies with the top value. • Most of the companies in the NASDAQ index are high-tech companies. • When the stock averages rise, it means the stock market is doing well.

Investors look at trends over a length of time.

The DJIA is used in stock exchanges around the world.

CHARLES DOW Charles Dow created his stock average with Edward Jones. At the time, the stock market was not popular with investors. They thought it was risky. Dow wanted to change their minds. He showed them it was not as risky as they thought. He showed investors they could make money if they looked at stock market trends.

The Value of the Stock Market *Always Changes*

9

Stock market averages show how stocks are doing over time. Sometimes, stock prices trend up. This is called a bull market. Sometimes, stock market prices trend down. This is called a bear market. It is easiest to see these trends over long periods of time. This can be months or years.

On any given day, individual stock prices rise and fall. Sometimes stock prices change by just pennies. Other times stock prices rise and fall by much more. These changes in stock prices are called market **fluctuations**.

Usually, stock prices change slowly. There are times, though, when the stock market makes big changes in one day. October 19, 1987, was one day like that. Today, it is called Black Monday. On that day, the US stock market lost 22.6 percent of its value. Why did this happen? Financial experts are not sure. All major world markets had been dropping in value. Three of them had dropped by more than 40 percent. There were several military conflicts around the world. Stockbrokers were still learning how to use new computers. For some or all of these reasons, investors started panic selling.

Luckily, US stock markets regained half of their losses fairly quickly. Two years later, the markets had recovered totally.

$500 billion Amount of money lost on the DJIA on Black Monday, 1987.

After the 1987 crash, investors learned not to panic. The stock market eventually recovers. • Stock exchanges around the world now have "circuit breakers." • These "circuit breakers" make stock trading pause when prices go down too much.

A bull signals an upward trend in the market while a bear means a downward trend.

There Are No Guarantees in *the Stock Market*

10

Stock market investors can make a lot of money. But they can lose a lot of money, too. There are no guarantees in the stock market. But there are possibilities. And everyone who participates in the stock market has the same goal. They want to make money.

The stock market offers benefits to companies and investors. When investors buy stocks, they have the chance to make money. Companies use the money from investors to grow. The money also helps run their day-to-day business. Sometimes investors do not have to wait to sell their shares to make money. Some companies pay the investors **dividends**. The amount of the dividend is based on how much money the company has made. It also depends on how many shares an investor owns. Dividends are usually paid four times per year.

The main goal of the stock market is to make money.

7 Number of tech companies that outperformed in the stock market in 2023.

They are Microsoft, Apple, Nvidia, Amazon, Meta, Tesla, and Alphabet. • There were also companies in the 2023 market that lost a lot of value. • The seven worst were Pfizer, Chevron, Johnson and Johnson, Exxon Mobil, Bristol-Myers Squibb, NextEra Energy, and Moderna.

However, there are disadvantages to investing in the stock market. Buying and selling stocks is a gamble. No one knows for sure if they will make money. Sometimes, such as on Black Monday, stocks lose value before they can be sold. Sometimes companies lose money or go out of business. In those cases, investors lose.

People can lose thousands of dollars if they invest in the wrong stocks.

The Stock Market Can *Crash*

11

Rarely, the stock market makes a big drop in a short period of time. This is called a crash. A crash is different from normal market changes.

Imagine there are three companies who all sell jackets. Company A sells leather jackets. Company B sells denim ones. Company C sells nylon jackets. Many people buy the leather jackets. The denim jackets are less popular. The nylon jackets do not sell at all. Company C lowers its prices. After a while, people are not buying any jackets. Both Company A and B drop their prices as well. Still, no jackets sell. The companies panic. They really want to get rid of their supply of jackets. But no matter how low the prices are, no one buys them. Supply is much higher than demand. The companies' stock prices crash.

A similar scenario can happen with big stock exchanges. Many companies drop prices at the same time. There are more sellers than buyers. Supply is greater than demand. The value of stocks owned by investors drops. The stock market crashes. There were big crashes in 1929 and 1987. Smaller crashes occurred in 2001, 2008, and 2020.

23 Percentage the average price of stocks fell on the DJIA on October 29, 1929.

The stock market crash of 1929 started the Great **Depression**. • The Great Depression was worldwide. But the United States was hit the hardest. • About 13 million people lost their jobs.

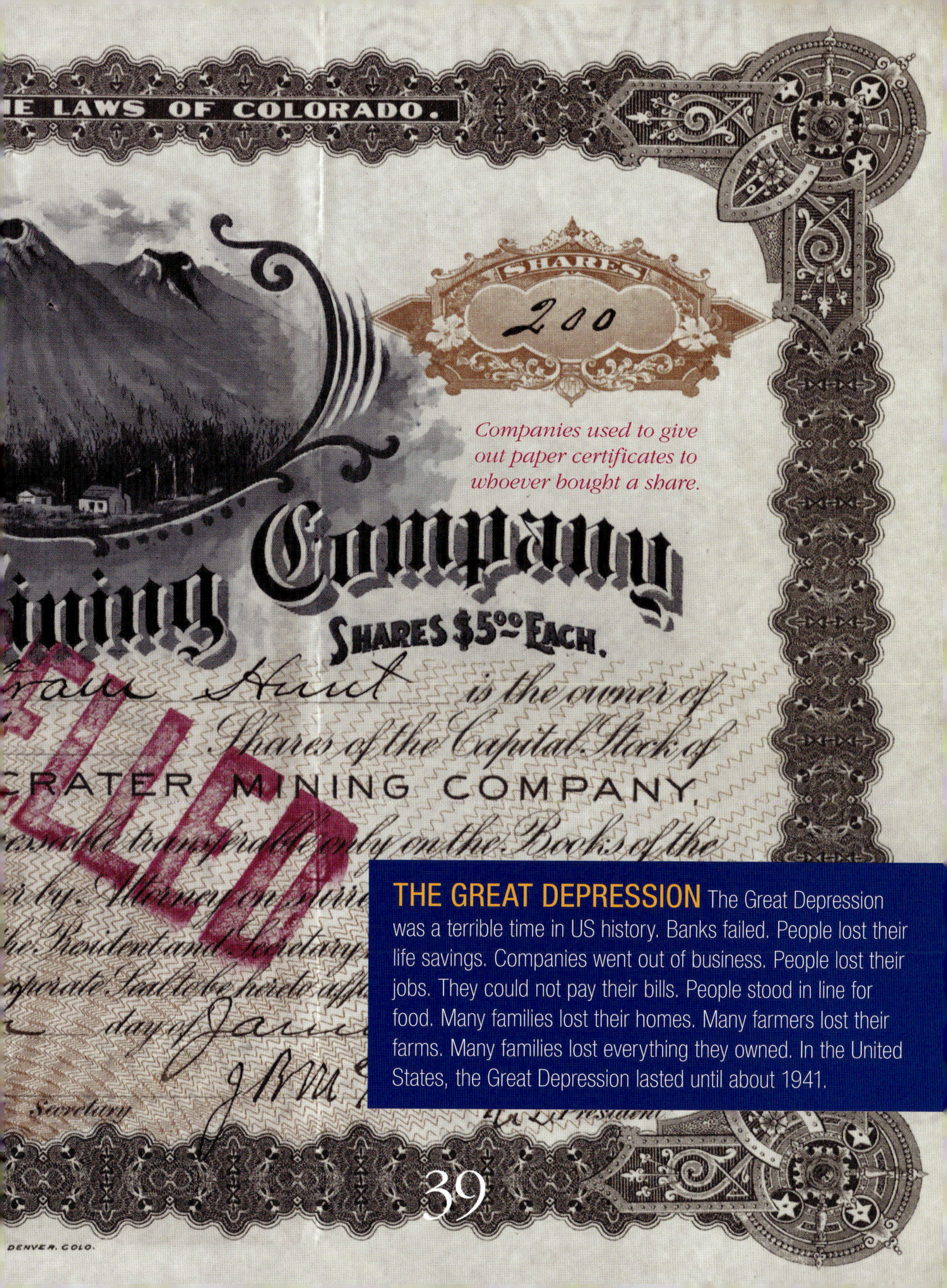

Companies used to give out paper certificates to whoever bought a share.

THE GREAT DEPRESSION The Great Depression was a terrible time in US history. Banks failed. People lost their life savings. Companies went out of business. People lost their jobs. They could not pay their bills. People stood in line for food. Many families lost their homes. Many farmers lost their farms. Many families lost everything they owned. In the United States, the Great Depression lasted until about 1941.

Laws Make Sure the Stock Market *Is Fair*

12

The stock market crash in 1929 was terrible. The US government knew it had to take action. It had to make the stock market fair for everyone. In 1934, the SEC was formed. The job of the SEC is to protect investors. It makes sure the US stock market is fair. The stock market is also monitored by the FBI.

Sometimes people involved in the stock market break the law. This is called securities **fraud**. It is a **white-collar crime**. One kind of securities fraud is stock fraud. This happens when brokers lie to investors. The brokers try to convince them to buy certain stocks. Another type of fraud is called insider trading. Sometimes someone gets private information about a company. This could be information about new products. It could be about prices. It could be about upcoming deals. They use this information to buy or

A famous photograph shows a worried mother during the Great Depression.

sell stocks and make money. It is okay to use public information but not private information.

A third type of fraud is called a Ponzi scheme. Legally, a company must pay dividends to investors from what it has earned. A Ponzi scheme is different. The company does not pay out anything. Instead, the first investors in the business are paid by the second investors. The second investors are paid by the third, and so on. The investors at the top of the pyramid make a lot of money. The investors at the bottom of the pyramid lose a lot of money.

$64 billion Amount of money investors lost in the biggest Ponzi scheme in US history.

It was run by Bernie Madoff, a money manager. • In 2009, he was sentenced to 150 years in prison. He had to pay back $170 billion. • Madoff died in prison in 2021. He was 82.

Ponzi schemes cause many people to lose money.

Fact

• Warren Buffet was born in 1930. He is considered the most successful investor of the 20th century. Buffet made thoughtful and smart investments over the years. Today, he runs Berkshire Hathaway. This company owns many smaller companies. In 2024, at age 93, Buffet was worth $136 billion. He has promised to donate 99 percent of all his money. As of 2024, he had donated more than $56 billion.

• The terms “bull market” and “bear market” have been around for a while. Examples of them appear in documents from the 18th century. People are not sure why these terms were chosen. Some think it is how the animals attack.
A bull market is a rising market. A bull attacks by moving its horns up.
A bear market is a falling market. A bear attacks by swiping its claws down.

Sheet

- Open outcry was the way stocks used to be traded. Traders met on the floor of the stock exchange. Buyers and sellers would try to find each other. There was often a lot of shouting and screaming. Today, most stock exchanges use computers. Advanced systems match up buyers and sellers. Open outcry still happens at the NYSE and the London Metal Exchange.

- Many victories are celebrated in New York City with parades. Ticker tape parades started in 1886. Ticker tape was a ribbon of paper. It came out of a ticker tape machine. Stock prices were recorded on it. Stockbrokers often worked in New York's tall buildings. They threw the ticker tape out the windows during parades. Ticker tape parades became very popular. Today, there are no more ticker tape machines. The city delivers confetti to the people in skyscrapers. They still throw it out the windows.

Glossary

audit
To check records or accounts for accuracy.

bond
An investment where the investor lends money to a company or government at a fixed interest rate.

depression
A period of time when there is low economic activity and high unemployment.

dividend
An amount of a company's profits given to investors.

fluctuation
An irregular shifting in the level, strength, or value of something.

fraud
The crime of using dishonest methods to take something valuable from another person.

free market
An economy in which prices are based on competition among private businesses and not controlled by a government.

investment
The act of using money to earn more money.

real estate
Land or buildings people purchase or invest in.

securities
Stock certificates, bond certificates, and other documents that prove ownership of an investment.

share
A part of a company an investor owns.

split
Dividing one stock share into multiple shares.

white-collar crime
Non-violent crimes committed by business or government officials for financial gains.

For More Information

Books

Green, Jonathan. *Stock Market Stars: A Beginner's Guide to Investing for Kids.* Sudbury, MA: Ebookit.com, 2024.

Hill, Christina. *The Stock Market in Infographics.* Ann Arbor, MI: Cherry Lake Press, 2023.

Websites

Kid's Money
www.kidsmoney.org/kids/investing/stock-market/

StockUp Kids
stockupkids.com/

The Stock Market Game
www.stockmarketgame.org

About the Author

Vicki Hayes has a master's degree in early childhood education and more than 30 years of experience teaching children of all ages. She currently works as a teacher and writer.

Index

Copyright © 2025 Black Rabbit Books. All rights reserved. No part of this book may be reproduced in any form without written permission from the publisher.

• Top Rank is an imprint of Black Rabbit Books. • Edited by Alissa Thielges | Designed by Danny Nanos • Photographs © Alamy Stock Photo/WENN, 44; Bridgeman Images/CSU Archives/Everett Collection, 16; Dreamstime/Brian Lerich, 13, Dmitry Rukhlenko, cover, Elliott Cowand Jr., 32, 33, 44, Fedecandoniphoto, 37, Fireflyphoto, 38–39, F11photo, 22, Httin, 12, Oleg Dudko, 34–35, RightFramePhotoVideo, 10, Sergey Galushko, 17, Tim Wolnitza, 32–33, 350jb, 11; Shutterstock/artichoke studio, 43, Belinda Pretorius, 48, Colinmthompson, 9, dee karen, 27, 28, gary yim, 45, Gorodenkoff, 29, Jolygon, 46–47, Kira_Yan, 31, leolintang, 2, 20, mapo_japan, 18–19, Mehaniq, 18, Mihai_Andritoiu, 14–15, Oleh11, 12, orhan akkurt, 4, Poznyakov, 23, 45, rvlsoft, 26, Tada Images, 8, Vershinin89, 6, Volodymyr Nikitenko, 5, wantanddo, 40, 41, worradirek, 36, zignal_88, 2–3, 7, 1st footage, 25 • Printed in China

Library of Congress Cataloging-in-Publication Data Names: Hayes, Vicki, author. | Title: 12 things to know about the stock market / Vicki Hayes. | Description: Mankato, MN: Black Rabbit Books, [2025] | Series: Today's headlines | Includes bibliographical references and index. | Ages 9–13 | Grades 4–6 | Identifiers: LCCN 2024026482 | ISBN 9781645823896 (library binding) | ISBN 9781645824114 (paperback) | ISBN 9781645824336 (ebook) Subjects: LCSH: Stock exchanges—Juvenile literature. | Economics—Juvenile literature. | Classification: LCC HG4553 .H38 2025 | DDC 332.64/2—dc23/eng/20240716 | LC record available at https://lccn.loc.gov/2024026482